ENERGY

EARTH'S CLIMATE CHANGE

Carbon Dioxide Overload

D1073619

James Bow

CRABTREE
Publishing Company
www.crabtreebooks.com

Crabtree Publishing Company

www.crabtreebooks.com

Author: James Bow

Editors: Sarah Eason, Jen Sanderson, and Shirley Duke

Proofreader: Katie Dicker and Wendy Scavuzzo

Editorial director: Kathy Middleton

Design: Paul Myerscough and Geoff Ward

Cover design: Paul Myerscough

Photo research: Sarah Eason and Jen Sanderson

Prepress technician: Margaret Amy Salter

Print coordinator: Margaret Amy Salter

Consultant: Richard Spilsbury, degree in Zoology, 30 years as an author and editor of educational science books

Written and produced for Crabtree Publishing by Calcium Creative

Library and Archives Canada Cataloguing in Publication

Bow, James, 1972-, author
    Earth's climate change : carbon dioxide overload / James Bow.

(Next generation energy)
Includes index.
Issued in print and electronic formats.
ISBN 978-0-7787-1978-6 (bound).--
ISBN 978-0-7787-2001-0 (paperback).--
ISBN 978-1-4271-1636-9 (pdf).--
ISBN 978-1-4271-1628-4 (html)

    1. Atmospheric carbon dioxide--Environmental aspects--Juvenile literature. 2. Carbon dioxide--Environmental aspects--Juvenile literature. 3. Atmospheric carbon dioxide--Juvenile literature. 4. Carbon dioxide--Juvenile literature. 5. Carbon dioxide mitigation--Juvenile literature. I. Title.

QC879.8.B69 2015   j363.738'74   C2015-903210-5
                                                C2015-903211-3

Library of Congress Cataloging-in-Publication Data

Bow, James, author.
 Earth's climate change : carbon dioxide overload / James Bow.
    pages cm. -- (Next generation energy)
 Includes index.
 ISBN 978-0-7787-1978-6 (reinforced library binding : alk. paper)
 -- ISBN 978-0-7787-2001-0 (pbk. : alk. paper)
 -- ISBN 978-1-4271-1636-9 (electronic pdf : alk. paper)
 -- ISBN 978-1-4271-1628-4 (electronic html : alk. paper)
 1. Greenhouse effect, Atmospheric--Juvenile literature. 2. Carbon dioxide--Juvenile literature. 3. Global warming--Juvenile literature. 4. Climatic changes--Juvenile literature. I. Title.

QC912.3.B69 2016
363.738'74--dc23
                    2015020964

Crabtree Publishing Company

www.crabtreebooks.com   1-800-387-7650

Printed in Canada/082015/BF20150630

Published in Canada
Crabtree Publishing
616 Welland Ave.
St. Catharines, Ontario
L2M 5V6

Published in the United States
Crabtree Publishing
PMB 59051
350 Fifth Avenue, 59th Floor
New York, New York 10118

Published in the United Kingdom
Crabtree Publishing
Maritime House
Basin Road North, Hove
BN41 1WR

Published in Australia
Crabtree Publishing
3 Charles Street
Coburg North
VIC, 3058

Contents

What Is Global Climate Change?

You may have heard about global warming, but it should really be called global climate change. You may not know what these terms really mean, other than they could be bad for planet Earth, and they might have something to do with our use of energy. This is mostly true, but the problem is a little more complicated. To understand global climate change, we must first understand energy.

Energy is the ability to do work. We use energy to move our bodies. We also use it to turn on lights and power refrigerators. Energy drives automobiles and other vehicles. Energy has many different forms. For example, **mechanical energy** moves things using simple machines such as levers, ramps, and pulleys. **Chemical energy** is released when different substances react with each other. **Nuclear energy** is released by breaking apart **atoms**. Atoms are the smallest possible parts of a element. Heat and light are also forms of energy. Stored energy is called **potential energy** and moving energy is called **kinetic energy**.

Since 1970, our energy use has grown and our use of coal, oil, and natural gas (**methane**) has increased, too.

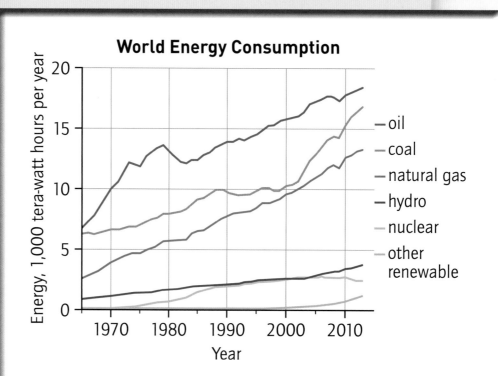

World Energy Consumption

Energy, 1,000 tera-watt hours per year

— oil
— coal
— natural gas
— hydro
— nuclear
— other renewable

Year

Where Does Energy Go After We Use It?

Energy cannot be created or destroyed, it can only be transformed, or changed, from one form to another. Even so, it can be hard to change energy back to its original form. For example, once some fuels are transformed, they are gone. These fuels are called **nonrenewable** energy sources. **Renewable** energy, such as wind or the Sun's heat, is not used up so easily.

When we burn fuel such as oil or gasoline, the energy inside is released as heat and harmful or poisonous by-products, called **pollutants**. **Carbon dioxide**, which is a gas molecule made up of a carbon atom joined with two oxygen atoms, is one such pollutant. This gas is causing most of the concern about global climate change.

The Sun provides Earth with heat and light. There are ways to use that heat and light to **generate**, or make, electricity.

REWIND

While people today worry about the pollution from burning fuels such as oil and gasoline, oil was once seen as a benefit to the **environment**. Before there were automobiles, people used horses to get around. In 1900, there were as many as 3.5 million horses in cities across the United States, and up to 175,000 horses in New York City alone. With all that manure to handle, the exhaust fumes of automobiles were an improvement… until the number of vehicles increased, along with their impact on the environment. What would New York City be like today if all those cars were replaced by horses?

The Greenhouse Effect

Carbon dioxide, along with methane and water vapor, are greenhouse gases. In the atmosphere, these gases let the Sun's energy pass through to Earth's surface, but they stop that energy from being reflected off the surface and back into space. This process is known as the greenhouse effect because, like the glass sides of a greenhouse, greenhouse gases trap heat in Earth's atmosphere, which warms the planet.

The greenhouse effect is a good thing. Without it, the average world temperature would be 0°Fahrenheit (-18°Celcius). All the water on the planet would freeze and we would die. The problem comes when we have too much greenhouse gas. Then, too much of the Sun's energy is trapped and Earth becomes too hot.

The Carbon Cycle

The amount of carbon dioxide in the atmosphere naturally rises and falls through a pattern called the **carbon cycle**. Plants absorb carbon dioxide in a process called **photosynthesis**. In photosynthesis, plants break up the carbon dioxide into carbon, which they use to grow, and oxygen, which is released into the atmosphere. Animals that eat the plants also absorb that carbon.

Trees help balance the amount of carbon dioxide in the atmosphere. They absorb carbon dioxide and release oxygen.

When plants and animals decay, the carbon is returned to the atmosphere as carbon dioxide and methane. However, if the plant or animal is buried, the carbon can be removed from the atmosphere for a long time.

Carbon that is buried and stored in forests and marshes is called a **carbon sink**. If a sink is buried under tons of rock, it is removed from the carbon cycle for millions of years. Stuck underground in the right conditions, a carbon sink can become a **fossil fuel**. Coal, oil, and natural gas are fossil fuels.

Some scientists believe that Earth's atmosphere lost so much carbon dioxide 650 million years ago, that most of the surface froze. They call this "snowball Earth."

REWIND

Starting in 1492, diseases brought by European explorers killed up to 50 million Native Americans. The devastation to their population left fewer people to farm and live on the land across North America. The farms regrew into forests. The new trees absorbed more carbon dioxide. Along with increased volcanic activity and other factors, the forests lowered global average temperatures, resulting in the "Mini Ice Age." Today, forests are being cut down at an alarming rate—the Amazon rain forest has lost 17 percent of its trees in the past 50 years. How could this cutting down of forests, or **deforestation**, alter the greenhouse effect?

Energy and Climate Change

Coal produces around 29 percent of the world's energy, and more than 40 percent of the world's electricity. Oil provides 37 percent of the world's energy. Without coal and oil, there would be far less electricity to power homes. Electricity would also be a lot more expensive to buy. Transportation would be a problem because automobiles, planes, and trains would not be powered. Machines would not work either.

Ancient Fuel

Along with methane, coal and oil are **hydrocarbons**. These are molecules made up of carbon and hydrogen atoms, which come from the remains of plants and animals that died millions of years ago. Then, as now, plants absorbed carbon dioxide through their leaves, and used sunshine and water to turn the gas into a food through photosynthesis. Over millions of years, plant-eaters such as dinosaurs died and were buried underground, taking their carbon with them. These plants and animals rotted under millions of tons of rock, and their carbon and water molecules combined to become oil or coal.

The Sun's heat is trapped by Earth's atmosphere. When too much carbon dioxide is added to the atmosphere, even more heat is trapped, and our planet warms up.

We have already talked about how carbon dioxide and methane are greenhouse gases that trap the Sun's heat in the atmosphere. When oil and coal are burned, they release back into the atmosphere carbon dioxide that was removed from the atmosphere millions of years ago. The atmosphere already contains carbon dioxide. When more carbon dioxide is added, it is enough to tip our atmosphere out of balance and make the world warmer. This is called global climate change.

In some cities of the world, so many gases are given off by factories and vehicles that the air is heavily polluted. Many people in these places wear masks when they go outside to help protect themelves from the polluted air.

The Energy Future: You Choose

Wind and solar power can provide **alternative** sources of energy that do not add to climate change. However, some people argue that wind and solar power technology is a long way from replacing the amount of energy produced by coal and oil. They say using alternative forms of energy will just make coal and oil more expensive to buy. Others argue that we should try to reduce our use of coal and oil, and we should accept paying more for energy. What do you think? Support your answers with examples from this book and other research.

A History of Climate Change

Petra was a city founded in the Jordanian desert around 300 BCE. It grew rich as a trading hub between the Roman Empire and the Middle East. Petra's citizens carved buildings into the cliffs which still stand today. Petra and Rome benefited from the Roman Warm Period. This was a period of warm weather from 250 BCE to 400 CE that lengthened growing seasons and put more food on the table. Rome grew rich and built an empire.

Then, in around 400 CE, the climate suddenly cooled, possibly as a result of dust from a large volcanic eruption that blocked the Sun's heat. Around the world, the years that followed were a period of **drought** and famine. The Roman Empire weakened and fell. Not only did Petra lose a trading partner, but its own climate also became a lot drier. The city was abandoned soon after.

The city of Petra lay abandoned and hidden from Europeans for centuries, until John Lewis Burckhardt discovered it in August 1812.

Planning Ahead

Climate change has destroyed civilizations throughout history. The Anasazi of New Mexico abandoned their cliff dwellings because of a 50-year-long drought that started in 1130 CE. There is also evidence that climate change forced early humans out of Africa because there was not enough food for everyone.

It is hard to predict the weather, but people depend on it to be stable enough so that farmers can plan to plant the following year's crops. For example, people in Canadian cities cope with snow better than people in the southern United States because they expect snow to fall and have equipment to clear it. However, people in most places do not handle unexpected weather very well, and with climate change, unexpected weather becomes more common.

All Change

Could climate change lead us to abandon our own cities? In the 1930s, drought and dust storms in the American Midwest forced people to abandon their farms and look for work in California. The drought ended in 1939. The consequences might have been disastrous had it not.

FAST FORWARD

In 2008, scientists at the Geological Society of London, England, proposed that Earth was entering a new **geological age**. They called it the Anthropocene, meaning "human age." These scientists argue that humanity has had as much impact on Earth as the asteroid strike that hit the planet 66 million years ago and helped drive dinosaurs to extinction. Do you think that is a fair comparison? How are human changes different from an asteroid strike?

Without rain, plants die and the fertile soil they hold blows away, leaving no food for animals to graze on.

Climate Change

During the winters of 2014 and 2015, a **polar vortex** pushed warm air from the Pacific Ocean north into Alaska. This forced Arctic air south to cover the eastern part of North America. It drove temperatures to record lows. In February 2015, Senator James Inhofe tossed a snowball onto the floor of the US Senate, claiming the snow was proof that global climate change was not happening.

However, what Senator Inhofe did not mention was that the city of Nome, Alaska, near the Arctic Circle, had temperatures of 35.6°F (2°C). The average low temperature there in February is 0°F (–18°C). Outside of eastern Canada and the northeastern United States, it was the warmest February on record.

In the winter of 2014, New York City (right) saw a record amount of snow. In 2015, Boston was covered by more than 9 feet (2.7 m) of snow, causing great disruption.

Hot Makes Cold

Around the world, the climate varies. Climate is the normal weather conditions that an area has over a long period of time. Climate is not affected only by the heat of the Sun. Winds, ocean currents, and mountains all have a part to play in determining whether a place is warm or cold, or wet or dry. For example, the United Kingdom and northern Europe are much warmer than Newfoundland and Labrador, even though both are at the same **latitude**, or distance from the **equator**. This is because the Gulf Stream ocean current in the Atlantic pulls warm water from the Caribbean to Europe, bringing warmer weather. These details affect how each place will change as, on average, the world warms up.

Global climate change could mean certain areas can get wetter. In winter, that means more snow will fall to the ground.

REWIND

The theory that human activity has caused climate change has been accepted by most of the scientific community. However, climate change "skeptics" seek to cast doubts about this **consensus**. They raise points that sound as though they go against the theory, but those points do not stand up to scientific tests. For example, they argue that average temperatures have not risen since 1998. However, 1998 was an unusually warm year, even with the warming trend. Measuring temperatures from 1997 or 1999 shows that global average temperatures are still increasing. Why do you think climate change skeptics might want to raise doubts about a scientific consensus?

Using Energy in the Past

If coal and oil contribute so much to global climate change, why do we still use these energy sources? This is because the benefits of these fuels are so easy to see and the consequences, or results, of using them are so difficult to accept.

Thousands of years ago, humans learned how to make fire and life became a lot easier. They could cook food, keep warm at night, and burn away grasses and trees that could hide dangerous wild animals. To make fire, people cut down trees or cut peat, which is made from rotted plant materials, out of bogs. This source of energy is called **biomass**. Although burning biomass released carbon dioxide into the atmosphere, it was done on a much smaller scale compared to today, and it did not upset the environment.

REWIND

Before people learned to use oil from the ground, they hunted whales for oil. Whale oil was used to light lamps and make candles, soap, and makeup. Through most of the 1800s, whaling ships killed so many whales that some species were brought to extinction, or close to it. If people had not figured out how to use oil from the ground, what could have happened to the whales? How might this have affected people?

A Need for Balance

There were places in the world, however, where people's activities changed the environment. One example is Easter Island in the Pacific Ocean, west of Peru. The island is famous for its stone statues of human heads, called Moai. When Polynesian settlers arrived around 1000 CE, the island had trees and fertile soil. The settlers cleared the trees to create farmland, and by 1600, 15,000 people lived on the island. Then, the last trees were cut down. By 1722, the population had dropped to around 2,000 people. Without the trees, the soil became poor and not enough food could be grown to feed everyone.

Easter Island's Moai are evidence of a civilization that has largely vanished as a result of deforestation.

Better Energy

Elsewhere, people were luckier. As technology developed, they discovered better energy sources that were able to do many tasks.

It is natural for people to want their lives to improve. If they find a way to put more food on the table or make work easier, they embrace it, especially if they do not realize that the energy taken to do it will not always be available.

This engraving shows whale hunting in the 1800s.

The Industrial Revolution

In 1698, English inventor Thomas Savery figured out how to use the pressure of steam to drive a pump to suck water from a mine. In 1781, Scotland's James Watt made a steam engine that could turn a wheel. This invention caused a change in how things were made. This period of change became known as the **Industrial Revolution**. Suddenly, people built machines to transport passengers and goods. Factories produced enough goods in a day that before would take weeks to make.

The ability to produce things faster and cheaper made a lot of people very wealthy. It made things such as food cheaper to buy. People were able to buy more, so they wanted more. This created a demand for more things than the machines could make. People started moving to cities, and away from farms where machines were doing more of the people's work anyway. In cities, they took work in factories.

Coalbrookdale by Night by Philip James de Louterbourg was painted in 1801. The painting shows Madeley Wood (or Bedlam) Furnaces, which were used to smelt iron, removing it from ore, in the 1700s.

The Power Behind Machines

Fuel had to be burned to provide the energy required to power the machines. The demand for wood, then for coal and oil, increased dramatically. More machines were needed to help search for coal and oil. The increase in machines meant more goods and more money spent. This, in turn, meant a demand for more machines to make more goods, and more money was made.

In 1800, during the Industrial Revolution, carbon dioxide took up 280 parts per million (ppm) of Earth's atmosphere. By burning fossil fuels, this increased to more than 315 ppm by 1960, and over 400 ppm by 2015.

This photograph shows a child worker in the Chace Cotton Mill in Vermont. The demand for fuel to run machines such as those in mills, led to a huge increase in carbon dioxide output.

The Energy Future: You Choose

The Industrial Revolution changed the world, but was the change for the better? The factories and farm equipment made food and goods cheaper, but also put some people out of work and increased pollution. At the same time, it created new jobs in cities, and new technology that helped clean up the pollution. Is change unavoidable? How can it be managed to prevent bad things from happening? Discuss your answers and support your ideas with examples. What part did technology play in these changes?

The Agricultural Revolution

In addition to factories in growing cities, people's use of fossil-fuel-powered machines changed the way they farmed, creating an **agricultural** "revolution." Plows that were pulled by horses could be pulled by tractors. Harvests that had to be cut by hand were cut by combines. The result was more and cheaper food. This allowed the world's population to grow and the population growth increased the demand for food.

Irrigation allows people to farm in the desert, as seen here in the Sahara. This helps supply food, but a lot of greenhouse gas emissions can come from this type of farming.

Sowing Environmental Problems

The new agricultural methods contributed to global climate change in many ways, such as from burning fossil fuels to power farm equipment. The demand for food pushed people to build more farms, cutting down forests that were taking carbon dioxide out of the atmosphere. **Irrigation** pulled more water from the ground, draining reservoirs and making areas more prone to drought. Some **fertilizers** were also made by extracting chemicals from fossils fuels such as oil, adding more carbon dioxide to the atmosphere. The number of livestock increased and its **excrement**, or waste, caused an increase in another greenhouse gas: methane.

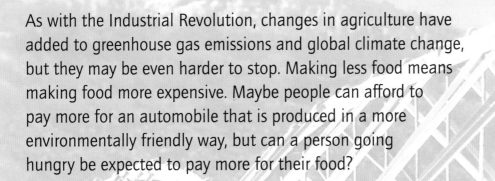

As with the Industrial Revolution, changes in agriculture have added to greenhouse gas emissions and global climate change, but they may be even harder to stop. Making less food means making food more expensive. Maybe people can afford to pay more for an automobile that is produced in a more environmentally friendly way, but can a person going hungry be expected to pay more for their food?

Despite all the food that is grown today, areas of the world still suffer famine. The question of how we can farm responsibly becomes difficult to answer when people need food to eat.

The Energy Future: You Choose

Irrigation makes farms possible in places that are dry, but these farms use up a lot of energy and water and add to the greenhouse effect. Without the farms, however, there would be a lot less to eat and food would be more expensive. Are people willing to pay more for the food they eat to make sure it is grown in an environmentally sustainable way? The world's population today is seven billion, and it could rise as high as nine billion by 2050. Can enough food be grown for everyone and the environment still be protected? Discuss and support your reasons why with examples and evidence from the book. Include ways technology might play a part.

The Developing World

While many agree fewer fossil fuels should be used, this becomes a problem when the developing world is expected to follow the same rules. The Industrial Revolution did not happen all at once. Countries such as China, Indonesia, and Brazil are just now developing more factories. Their standard of living is improving, so they use more fossil fuel.

In 2010, North America, the European Union, Japan, and Australia contributed over one third of the world's greenhouse gas emissions, even though they make up fewer than 20 percent of the world's population. If more countries industrialize, instead of 20 percent of the population emitting most of the greenhouse gases, 40 percent of the population will do so at the same rate. The environmental consequences of this would be disastrous. However, limiting the use of fossil fuels punishes countries that have not emitted many greenhouse gases to date, and prevents them from raising their standards of living.

Many people in the developing world are poorer than most in the developed world and they use far less energy. Given that developing countries want to grow in the way developed countries have grown, does the developed world have any right to say no?

Fighting the Greenhouse Effect

One way to deal with the increase in emissions in developing countries is to use carbon credits. In 1999, 84 countries signed the **Kyoto Protocol**. They promised to reduce global greenhouse emissions. The idea was to cap the amount of carbon dioxide each country could produce. Developed countries would hit this cap quickly, but developing countries, which had not fully industrialized, would have emissions to spare. They could sell these spare emissions as credits to industrialized countries. Putting a price on carbon dioxide emissions may encourage people to invest in alternative fuel sources.

The United States alone used 137 billion gallons (519 billion liters) of gasoline in 2014. What would happen if the rest of the world's countries begin to drive as many cars as those driven in the United States?

The Energy Future: You Choose

Most countries have not lived up to their commitments to cut emissions under the Kyoto Protocol. The problem can be described by a story called the *Tragedy of the Commons*. In this story, 10 herders with 10 cows each share a piece of land that can graze 100 cows. If one herder adds one cow to his herd, he will gain in wealth, while the other herders lose only a little land ... as long as he is the only one to do it. But if everyone thinks the same way, then the land dies from **overgrazing**. Overgrazing is when animals eat so much that the vegetation can't grow back fast enough. How can the rules be enforced when there is reason to cheat?

21

Fixing the Carbon Problem

The increase in the levels of carbon dioxide in the atmosphere since 1800 might be causing global climate change. Could the problem be solved by putting that carbon dioxide back into the ground it came from? Scientists are looking at ways to do this.

Carbon dioxide is naturally taken from the air by processes such as photosynthesis. Planting trees to replace chopped-down forests and restoring wetlands will help reduce carbon dioxide in the atmosphere, but it will not solve the entire problem. Fertilizing the oceans to encourage blooms of plankton could also pull carbon dioxide from the atmosphere, but we do not know how this would affect the marine ecosystem. Scientists are looking at substances that could absorb carbon dioxide and lock it away.

Global climate change is already melting sea ice in the Arctic, making it difficult for polar bears to move about.

Putting It Back Where It Came From

The natural methods of absorbing carbon dioxide work for only a short period. The idea of taking carbon dioxide and pumping it back into the ground has been around since 1972, when it was used as a means to add pressure to oil reservoirs to pump out more oil. As the underground reservoirs have held oil for millions of years, surely they could do the same with carbon dioxide gas?

However, gas flows more easily than oil, and the used reservoirs have been punctured and weakened through drilling. Leaks have already happened. For example, a pipeline in Netherlands carrying carbon dioxide burst and released enough gas to kill a number of nearby ducks. Carbon dioxide is poisonous in large quantities and a large leak could kill people.

Pipelines that carry carbon dioxide can sometimes leak into the surrounding environment, which can be disastrous for nearby wildlife and plants.

FAST FORWARD

In the permanently frozen soil layer of the Arctic permafrost, millions of tons of methane and carbon dioxide are locked out of the carbon cycle and the greenhouse effect. One of the worries about global climate change is that the world could heat up enough to melt the permafrost, releasing its methane and carbon dioxide into the atmosphere. Mysterious craters in the Siberian **permafrost** may be evidence that this is already happening. Can people reduce their greenhouse gas emissions enough to stop global climate change? What else can they do to lower carbon dioxide levels in the atmosphere?

Life Without Coal and Oil?

People use fossil fuels for so much of their energy, simply deciding to stop using these fuels is difficult. There are other sources of energy that can be used. These include the power of the Sun, the wind, and even Earth itself. These sources are not environmentally damaging and are renewable. Although the technology to use this energy is improving, it has not advanced enough to make alternative energy sources reliable enough to replace fossil fuels.

For a certain kind of energy to be useful, it has to be easy to find, easy to carry, and easy to put to use. In spite of the environmental problems of fossil fuels, and the fact they are a nonrenewable resource, until alternative technologies improve, fossil fuels are still the cheapest and easiest way to make machines work, and to heat buildings.

Alternative energy sources are great for generating electricity that can power the lights of buildings. Powering a city's cars without fossil fuels, however, is more challenging.

Less Is More

Another possible solution to reduce greenhouse gases could be to try to use less energy. This is called **conservation**. Instead of driving, people could walk more often or take public transportation. They could turn off the lights when they are not being used. However, some steps are harder to take than others. For the past 70 years, cities across North America have been designed with the automobile in mind. Giving up driving to walk or taking public transportation generally makes a trip take longer. Having farms or factories use cleaner energies also makes things, including food more costly.

New ways to use energy sustainably must be found to ensure that people in the developing world can live as well as those in the developed world.

The Energy Future: You Choose

Can people grow fuel? Ethanol is a fuel that can be made from crops such as corn. Growing crops does not add carbon dioxide to the atmosphere in the same way that fossil fuels do. However, growing fuel takes farm space away from other agriculture, making food more expensive. Fertilizers and the power needed to irrigate farms often come from fossil fuels. Can ethanol and other biofuels help reduce the dependence on fossil fuels? Are these biofuels a risk worth taking? Discuss your answers. What part might technology play in the changes and risks?

We Have Succeeded Before

There are big challenges ahead in dealing with global climate change and the world's dependence on fossil fuels. It is hard to imagine enough people changing their behavior to help the environment. However, people have changed their behavior before.

In the United States in the 1950s and the 1960s, pollution from vehicles and factories covered many cities with smog. The environment suffered and people's health was affected. In 1963 and 1970, the US government passed parts of the Clean Air Act. This law forced factories and car makers to reduce the amount of pollution that was in the air.

The industries said that the reduction was impossible and that it would raise prices and kill jobs, but the government and the people who elected them did not back down. Other countries such as Canada and the United Kingdom passed similar laws. As a result, the pollutants that caused smog were reduced, and the air quality of cities such as New York, London, and Toronto became much better.

Today, North American cities such as New York (below) have much cleaner air than they did before environmental regulations came into force 50 years ago.

Changing Technologies and Behaviors

Since the 1970s, a number of other pollutants have been reduced in our atmosphere. Governments passed laws to control environmental problems, but often people made the changes themselves. In the 1980s, there was great concern over **chlorofluorocarbons** (CFCs) and the damage they were doing to Earth's ozone layer. The ozone layer is part of the atmosphere that protects Earth from the Sun's **ultraviolet** rays. Public outcry convinced manufacturers of substances such as hairspray sold in **aerosol** containers to stop using CFCs. Industries reduced chemical emissions and acid rain is now less of a problem. Cars also burn less gasoline per mile (kilometer). We can continue to make changes to protect our planet's future.

Aerosol cans were popular until people realized how much damage the chemicals inside were doing to the environment.

FAST FORWARD

Some scientists have said that if we cannot stop global climate change, people may need to take big steps to protect themselves against the changing environment. Coastal cities, such as New York, might have to build dykes, or dams, and sea walls to be protected from rising sea levels. Cities near the equator might need to build domed enclosures to control the local climate. People may need to drop dust into clouds to make more rain or snow in drought-afflicted areas. Do you think these are good solutions to the problem? Give reasons for your answers. What ways can technology solve the problems?

Power Up!

Think of the energy that is needed to make the things you use in your day-to-day life. Can you live without these things? Fossil fuels have given us quality energy, but also great challenges. If we want a better life for ourselves and future generations, we need to meet those challenges head on.

What Can You Do?

The *Tragedy of the Common*, described on page 21, shows that the herders could have saved their land, but chose not to. People have the power to make choices that can reduce our use of fossil fuels and reduce global climate change. They can turn off lights when they are not using them. They can walk and take public transportation more often. They can choose to use solar, wind, or other alternative energy sources to power their homes.

People have changed their behavior before. They have improved city air and told businesses to stop harming the environment. Every step, however small, is still a step toward changing the world for the better.

Traveling by bicycle rather than by car is a great way to use fewer fossil fuels.

Activity

Around 50 CE, an inventor named Heron of Alexandria created the **aeolipile**. It was an engine that used heat and steam in much the same way as a steam engine does. In this experiment, you will create your own version of the aeolipile.

You Will Need:

- A pencil
- An empty, clean, cardboard milk carton
- Tape
- String
- A shoebox
- Old towels

Instructions

1. Use the pencil to poke a hole in each of the four sides of the milk carton, near the bottom left corner of each side. Place a piece of tape over each hole.
2. Poke a hole through the top of the carton and tie a piece of string to it.
3. Take the top off the shoebox and stand the box on one of its short ends. Place towels in the bottom of the box to catch the water.
4. Poke a small hole in the center of the other short end. Push the milk carton's string up through the hole from inside the box. Tie a knot large enough that it can't slip through the hole. Make sure the milk carton can turn freely.
5. Fill the carton with water.
6. Remove the tape from the holes.
7. Observe what happens.

What Happened?

The original aeolipile used a flame to heat water and produce steam. The steam pushed through the holes and made the aeolipile spin. This experiment shows how the device can work more safely, using water alone. Can you think of ways to make the aeolipile spin faster? What can you do to make it work with less water? How would that affect your machine's design?

Glossary

Please note: Some bold-faced words are defined where they appear in the text

aerosol A fine spray that hangs in the air when a substance is released under pressure

agricultural Of or relating to farming

alternative Something else that will achieve the results you want

atmosphere The layer of gases that surround Earth

biomass Organic material such as plants or animal waste

carbon cycle The continuous process in which carbon is exchanged between organisms and the environment

chlorofluorocarbons Molecules made from combining carbon, fluorine, and chlorine atoms

consensus When everyone or almost everyone agrees on something

conservation Slowing down or stopping the use of something so it will still be around in the future

drought A long period of time during which there is very little or no rain

environment The conditions of the area where something lives

equator An imaginary line around Earth at an equal distance from the North and South Poles

fertilizers Substances with nutrients added to soil to make plants grow

fossil fuels Energy sources made from the remains of plants and animals that died millions of years ago

geological age A measure of time determined by the formation of rocks, spanning millions to billions of years

greenhouse gases Gases in the atmosphere that contribute to the greenhouse effect

hydrocarbons Molecules from carbon and hydrogen atoms, usually made within plants or animals, which store a lot of energy and can release it when burned

Industrial Revolution A rapid change in which countries become more focused on using machines to make goods

irrigation Using water from rivers, lakes, or under ground to water crops in dry conditions

Kyoto Protocol A document signed by governments that commits them to reducing greenhouse gas emissions

methane A hydrocarbon molecule made up of one carbon atom and four hydrogen atoms, also known as a natural gas; It is a greenhouse gas.

nonrenewable Something that does not renew itself once it is used up

permafrost A layer of permanently frozen soil that is beneath the top layer of soil

photosynthesis A process in which plants use sunlight to make food from carbon dioxide and water, creating carbon atoms that they use to grow, and releasing oxygen into the atmosphere

polar vortex A pocket of extremely cold air, which sits over the polar region during winter

pollutants Materials that are introduced into the environment, and cause harmful or poisonous effects

renewable Something that renews itself once it is used

ultraviolet A type of energy from the Sun that cannot be seen by humans

Learning More

Find out more about alternative energy and global climate change.

Books

Gazlay, Suzy. *Re-Greening the Environment: Careers in Clean-up, Remediation, and Restoration* (Green-Collar Careers). Crabtree Publishing, 2012.

Hord, Colleen. *Clean and Green Energy*. Rourke, 2010.

Morgan, Sally. *Alternative Energy Sources* (Science at the Edge). Heinemann Library, 2009.

Oxlade, Chris. *Global Warming* (Mapping Global Issues). Smart Apple Media, 2012.

Snedden, Robert. *The Scientists Behind the Environment* (Sci-Hi). Heinemann-Raintree, 2011.

Websites

Learn about the environment, play games, and do eco-related activities at:
www.ecokids.ca

Learn more about energy, how to use it, and how to save it at:
www.energykids.eu

There are lessons about energy, how it is made, and how to stay safe at:
www.alliantenergykids.com

Learn more about Earth's climate and global climate change from NASA at:
http://climatekids.nasa.gov

Index